Worldwide Locations Trivia

Lance D. Williams

Published by Lance D. Williams, 2023.

While every precaution has been taken in the preparation of this book, the publisher assumes no responsibility for errors or omissions, or for damages resulting from the use of the information contained herein.

WORLDWIDE LOCATIONS TRIVIA

First edition. August 17, 2023.

ISBN: 979-8223572619

Written by Lance D. Williams.

Table of Contents

Introduction

One of my favorite things to do is travel to different locations and check out the area. Whether it's a small town in the middle of nowhere or going to a beautiful beach, there are so many unique scenes around the world, and I love learning about them. In this book, I wanted to give recognition to many places people may not know about and inspire them to learn more about certain places. If it's possible, hopefully you'll be able to visit some of the locations as well.

Beaches

1- Where is Grand Anse Beach?

(A)- San Clemente, California

(B)- Cape Town, South Africa

(C)- Perth, Australia

(D)- Saint George Parish, Grenada

2- This beach is in the town of Baunei.

(A)- Cala Goloritzé Beach

(B)- La Pelosa Beach

(C)- Marasusa Beach

(D)- Ponte dei Lapilli Beach

3- Which beach doesn't have black sand?

(A)- Tithal Beach

(B)- Cavendish Beach

(C)- Lafayette Beach

(D)- Kamari Beach

4- In the 2021 census, this place had a population of 9,303.

(A)- Manhattan Beach

(B)- Qualicum Beach

(C)- Qalansiyah Beach

(D)- Manzanillo Beach

5- This beach is in the province of La Altagracia.

(A)- Playa Zipolite

(B)- Playa Macao

(C)- Playa Punta Arenas

(D)- Playa de Gulpiyuri

6- In late July and early August, this beach has the Surf and Bodyboard Championships.

(A)- Monterrico Beach

(B)- Siesta Key Beach

(C)- Playa Zicatela

(D)- Kaihalulu Beach

7- Which beach isn't located in Australia?

(A)- Walvis Bay

(B)- Bells Beach

(C)- Turquoise Bay

(D)- Whitehaven Beach

8- This beach is in Ghana.

(A)- Labadi Beach

(B)- Elafonisi Beach

(C)- Saint-Pierre Beach

(D)- Porto Covo Beach

9- This beach is located on the shores of Lake Huron in Southwestern Ontario, Canada.

(A)- Eglin Beach Park

(B)- Hammonasset Beach State Park

(C)- Grand Bend Beach

(D)- Whitstable Beach

10- This is one of Lofoten's most famous beaches.

(A)- Playa de Sotavento de Jandia

(B)- Lovina Beach

(C)- Haukland Beach

(D)- Playa Juan Dolio

11- In 1906, this beach was created.

(A)- Doctor's Cave Beach

(B)- Coronado Beach

(C)- Sun Bay Beach

(D)- Treasure Cay Beach

12- This place is often referred to as the Golden Cape or Golden Horn.

(A)- Nosy Be

(B)- Keramas

(C)- Playa Negra

(D)- Zlatni Rat

13- Which beach is in Tahiti?

(A)- Muchangpo Beach

(B)- Sahara Beach

(C)- Horseshoe Bay Beach

(D)- Papenoo Beach

14- In 1931, this place was founded with the intention of turning a dune field into a timber plantation.

(A)- Hahei Beach

(B)- Baker Beach

(C)- Villa Gesell Beach

(D)- Plage de Palombaggia

15- Which place is in Westmoreland and Hanover parishes?

(A)- Myrtos Beach

(B)- Kalalau Beach

(C)- Astúrias Beach

(D)- Negril Seven Mile Beach

16- This place is also known as the "Rock Beach."

(A)- Praia del Vale dos Homens

(B)- Number One Beach

(C)- Praia da Rocha

(D)- Nissi Beach

17- This is a popular tourist spot because of a colony of African penguins which settled there in 1982.

(A)- Boulders Beach

(B)- Coligny Beach Park

(C)- Dueodde

(D)- Playa del Carmen Beach

18- Which one is sometimes referred to as "Smugglers Cove."

(A)- Kitsilano Beach

(B)- Navagio Beach

(C)- Laguna Beach

(D)- Dukhan Beach

19- This beach is one of only four green sand beaches in the world.

(A)- Papakolea Beach

(B)- Kovalam Beach

(C)- Kokkini Beach

(D)- Punta Maroma

20- In 2004, which one was included in a list of the Top 12 beaches in the world?

(A)- Englishman's Bay Beach

(B)- Barafundle Bay

(C)- Keem Bay

(D)- Playa de Levante

21- Which beach isn't in Florida?

(A)- Haulover Beach

(B)- Cocoa Beach

(C)- Long Sand Beach

(D)- Tigertail Beach

22- This beach is known for purple patches of sand.

(A)- Pfeiffer Beach

(B)- Macarella Beach

(C)- Ureki Beach

(D)- Benijo Beach

23- Which beach is in Jamaica?

(A)- Half Moon Caye

(B)- Pampelonne Beach

(C)- Punalu'u Beach

(D)- Hellshire Beach

24- This is a man-made beach, 800 meters in length and swimming is not permitted.

(A)- Myrtle Beach

(B)- Brackley Beach

(C)- Tokeh Beach

(D)- Odaiba Beach

25- This is the longest uninterrupted sandy seashore in the world.

(A)- Winnifred Beach

(B)- Praia do Cassino

(C)- Clearwater Beach

(D)- Bottom Bay

Beaches (Answers)

1- D

2- A

3- B

4- B

5- B

6- C

7- A

8- A

9- C

10- C

11- A

12- D

13- D

14- C

15- D

16- C

17- A

18- B

19- A

20- B

21- C

22- A

23- D

24- D

25- B

Capitals

26- What is the capital of Hungary?

(A)- Copenhagen

(B)- Prague

(C)- Budapest

(D)- Bridgetown

27- This place has officially been designated the "economic capital" of the Ivory Coast.

(A)- Abidjan

(B)- Bouaké

(C)- Yamoussoukro

(D)- Grand-Bassam

28- This is the capital of the island nation of Tuvalu.

(A)- Flying Fish Cove

(B)- Majuro

(C)- Funafuti

(D)- Honiara

29- Until 2006, this was the capital of Myanmar.

(A)- Monywa

(B)- Naypyidaw

(C)- Taungoo

(D)- Yangon

30- What is the capital of Qatar?

(A)- Doha

(B)- Al Jasrah

(C)- Fuwayrit

(D)- Mesaieed

31- According to the 2020 census, this capital had a population of 153,701.

(A)- Juneau, Alaska

(B)- Jackson, Mississippi

(C)- Carson City, Nevada

(D)- Charleston, West Virginia

32- This place is considered a second, unofficial capital of Germany.

(A)- Berlin

(B)- Düsseldorf

(C)- Hamburg

(D)- Bonn

33- Which place was selected as the first capital of Pakistan?

(A)- Lahore

(B)- Rawalpindi

(C)- Islamabad

(D)- Karachi

34- Ciudad de la Paz is currently under construction and will become the new capital of this place when complete.

(A)- Equatorial Guinea

(B)- Åland Islands

(C)- Oranjestad

(D)- Suva

35- Which place isn't the capital?

(A)- Port of Spain

(B)- Havana

(C)- Beijing

(D)- Petoskey

36- From 1914 to 1991, this was the capital of Nigeria.

(A)- Enugu

(B)- Lagos

(C)- Abuja

(D)- Ibadan

37- On April 21, 1782, this place was founded as a capital.

(A)- New Delhi

(B)- London

(C)- Bangkok

(D)- Kingston

38- This capital has a population of more than 2.8 million.

(A)- São Tomé

(B)- Tegucigalpa

(C)- Yaoundé

(D)- Stockholm

39- Which place doesn't have a capital in South America?

(A)- Sucre

(B)- Ankara

(C)- Fortaleza

(D)- Cayenne

40- As of 2022, this capital has a population of 437,811.

(A)- Tallinn

(B)- Kingstown

(C)- Jakarta

(D)- Luhansk

41- In 1792, this place became the capital.

(A)- Raleigh, North Carolina

(B)- Montpelier, Vermont

(C)- Atlanta, Georgia

(D)- Frankfort, Kentucky

42- This is one of the smallest capitals with a population of less than a thousand people.

(A)- Nukuʻalofa, Tonga

(B)- Kathmandu, Nepal

(C)- Hamilton, Bermuda

(D)- Managua, Nicaragua

43- In 2017, this capital city had a population of 433,249 and the metro area had 2,145,527.

(A)- Madrid, Spain

(B)- Hagåtña, Guam

(C)- Moscow, Russia

(D)- Beirut, Lebanon

44- The capital of Kazakhstan from 1929 to 1997 was ....

(A)- Taraz

(B)- Almaty

(C)- Shymkent

(D)- Astana

45- This is the capital of Liberia.

(A)- Mbombcla

(B)- Monrovia

(C)- Dodoma

(D)- Casablanca

Capitals (Answers)

26- C

27- A

28- C

29- D

30- A

31- B

32- D

33- D

34- A

35- D

36- B

37- C

38- C

39- B

40- A

41- A

42- C

43- D

44- B

45- B

National Parks

46 - What is the oldest national park in New Zealand?

(A)- Tongariro National Park

(B)- Castel National Park

(C)- Virachey National Park

(D)- Kubah National Park

47 - This park has an underwater cave system that is one of the longest of its kind in the world.

(A)- Lucayan National Park

(B)- Namib-Naukluft Park

(C)- Black Canyon of the Gunnison National Park

(D)- Kings Canyon National Park

48- This National Park was the first in Costa Rica in 1955.

(A)- Rincón de la Vieja National Park

(B)- San Lucas Island National Park

(C)- Poás Volcano National Park

(D)- La Amistad International Park

49- Which national park isn't in Germany?

(A)- Acadia National Park

(B)- Black Forest National Park

(C)- Berchtesgaden National Park

(D)- Jasmund National Park

50- Cliffs in this park reach 5,380 ft.

(A)- Solonga National Park

(B)- Pelican Cays Land and Sea Park

(C)- Madidi National Park

(D)- Basaseachic Falls National Park

51- This national park was established in 1978.

(A)- Yangmingshan National Park

(B)- Setonaikai National Park

(C)- Iguazú National Park

(D)- Kainji National Park

52- In July 1975, this place became the first legally established national park in Dominica.

(A)- Lake Clark National Park and Preserve

(B)- Alto Cariri National Park

(C)- Cordillera Azul National Park

(D)- Morne Trois Pitons National Park

53- This park was disestablished in 2014.

(A)- Laguna de Tacarigua National Park

(B)- Tu Urewera National Park

(C)- Hundred Islands National Park

(D)- Valley of Flowers National Park

54- It's estimated that there's at least 700 species of plants in this national park.

(A)- Alkhabay National Park

(B)- Crater Lake National Park

(C)- Guadeloupe Mountains National Park

(D)- Pindus National Park

55- Out of 22 national parks, this is the only one not managed by the Korea National Park Service.

(A)- Hallasan National Park

(B)- Bukhansan National Park

(C)- Jirisan National Park

(D)- Wolchulsan National Park

56- This national park is known for having giant lizards.

(A)- Yellowstone National Park

(B)- Borjomi-Kharagauli National Park

(C)- Bahia de Loreto National Park

(D)- Komodo National Park

57- This national park has 32 species of mammal, including most of the world's 65 remaining golden-headed langurs, the world's most endangered primate.

(A)- Cát Bà National Park

(B)- Ñacunday National Park

(C)- Söderåsen National Park

(D)- Iguaçu National Park

58- This park protects 2,309 hectares where elevations range from 9,186 to 11,260 feet.

(A)- Irazú Volcano National Park

(B)- Big Bend National Park

(C)- Addo Elephant National Park

(D)- Denali National Park and Preserve

59- Currently Bangladesh has this many national parks.

(A)- 18

(B)- 28

(C)- 38

(D)- 48

60- This park was placed on the World Heritage Site Tentative List in 2016.

(A)- North Cascades National Park

(B)- Gran Paradiso National Park

(C)- Central Karakoram National Park

(D)- Shey Phoksundo National Park

61- Which one was the first national park in Kerala?

(A)- Eravikulam National Park

(B)- Congaree National Park

(C)- Jaragua National Park

(D)- Shenandoah National Park

62- In 1986, this place was declared a national park by Presidential Decree No. 86-1283.

(A)- Anyuysky National Park

(B)- Hawai'i Volcanoes National Park

(C)- Wicklow Mountains National Park

(D)- Korup National Park

63- This park has more than 1,000 flowering plant species, including 163 species of trees and 104 ferns.

(A)- Indiana Dunes National Park

(B)- Bwindi Impenetrable National Park

(C)- Sequoia National Park

(D)- Mount Rainier National Park

64- In 2013, this park was extended to 25,000 acres.

(A)- Manovo-Gounda St. Floris National Park

(B)- Katavi National

(C)- Utrechtse Heuvelrug National Park

(D)- Pico da Neblina National Park

65- In 2017, which park had 304,408 visitors?

(A)- Augrabies Falls National Park

(B)- Virgina Islands National Park

(C)- Gates of the Arctic National Park and Preserve

(D)- Mombacho Volcano Natural Reserve

66- This park is one of the most remote and difficult to reach areas in Haiti.

(A)- Dolomiti Bellunesi National Park

(B)- Hamat Tiberias National Park

(C)- Lassen Volcanic National Park

(D)- Grande Colline National Park

67- Which one has 337,598 acres?

(A)- Canyonlands National Park

(B)- Tusheti National Park

(C)- Cúc Phương National Park

(D)- Exuma Cays Land and Sea Park

68- This was the first national park in the Atlantic provinces of Canada.

(A)- Voyageurs National Park

(B)- Los Tres Ojos National Park

(C)- Wasgamuwa National Park

(D)- Cape Breton Highlands National Park

69- Puong Cave is located at this park.

(A)- Port Campbell National Park

(B)- Ba Bể National Park

(C)- Stelvio National Park

(D)- Joshua Tree National Park

70- Established in 1990, this is the second largest in Guatemala.

(A)- Sierra del Lacandón National Park

(B)- Cañón del Río Blanco National Park

(C)- Bahia Portete - Kaurrele National Natural Park

(D)- Dilek Peninsula-Büyük Menderes Delta National Park

National Parks (Answers)

46- A

47- A

48- C

49- A

50- D

51- D

52- D

53- B

54- A

55- A

56- D

57- A

58- A

59- A

60- C

61- A

62- D

63- B

64- C

65- B

66- D

67- A

68- D

69- B

70- A

Counties & Regions

71- According to the 2020 census this is the second-most populous county in Montana, with a population of 118,960.

(A)- Gallatin County

(B)- Wabash County

(C)- Ouachita County

(D)- River Gee County

72- Which County was named for this Native American tribe.

(A)- Narok County

(B)- Ferdows County

(C)- Shoshone County

(D)- Waldo County

73- The Fabyan Windmill is on the National Register of Historic Places in this County.

(A)- Charlevoix County, Michigan

(B)- Rockbridge County, Virginia

(C)- Kane County, Illinois

(D)- Erie County, New York

74- The first U.S. County to reach a six-figure median household income was ....

(A)- Alachua County

(B)- Cape Girardeau County

(C)- Red River County

(D)- Fairfax County

75- How many counties are in Texas?

(A)- 227

(B)- 254

(C)- 314

(D)- 336

76- Which states don't call their first order administrative subdivisions counties?

(A)- Missouri and Arkansas

(B)- Alaska and Louisiana

(C)- Nevada and Montana

(D)- Wyoming and New Jersey

77- This place has the nickname "The County of Hidden Treasure."

(A)- Taita-Taveta County

(B)- Jämtland County

(C)- Kronoberg County

(D)- Västra Götaland County

78- In 2022, this County in Ireland had a population of 95,840

(A)- County Dublin

(B)- County Westmeath

(C)- County Kildare

(D)- County Wicklow

79- Which County isn't in Georgia?

(A)- Forsyth County

(B)- Cobb County

(C)- Oconee County

(D)- Allegan County

80- These 4 counties were created in Arizona in 1864.

(A)- Coconino, Graham, Grand Canyon Village and Queen Creek

(B)- Navajo, Pinal, Maricopa, and Cochise

(C)- Mohave, Pima. Yavapai and Yuma

(D)- Apache, Gila, La Paz, and Santa Cruz

81- On January 1, 2007, how many regions replaced counties in Denmark?

(A)- 5

(B)- 14

(C)- 20

(D)- 39

82- From 1873 to 1879 and again from 1883 to 1952, this was a County in South Dakota.

(A)- Hyde County

(B)- Armstrong County

(C)- Oglala Lakota County

(D)- Charles Mix County

83- This place has 314 land counties and 66 city counties.

(A)- Germany

(B)- Ukraine

(C)- Canada

(D)- Poland

84- This County area is 3,814 square miles.

(A)- Colfax County, New Mexico

(B)- Sandoval County, New Mexico

(C)- Rio Arriba County, New Mexico

(D)- Doña Ana County, New Mexico

85- The 2016 estimated population for this region in Brasil was 29.4 million.

(A)- North

(B)- Central-West

(C)- South

(D)- Northeast

86- Hereford and Worcester was an English non-metropolitan County created on April 1, 1974. What year was it abolished?

(A)- 1978

(B)- 1988

(C)- 1998

(D)- 2008

87- This County has three districts: The Central District, Tazeh Kand District, and Aslan Duz District.

(A)- Parsabad County

(B)- Mashhad County

(C)- Varzaqan County

(D)- Hamadan County

88- Samogitia is one of the five cultural regions of ....

(A)- Russia

(B)- Lithuania

(C)- India

(D)- Venezuela

89- This is a geographical and historical region in north-western Romania.

(A)- Crişana

(B)- Centre-Val de Loire

(C)- Cibao

(D)- Cantabria

90- This state currently has less than 3 counties.

(A)- Maine

(B)- Rhode Island

(C)- Delaware

(D)- Hawai'i

Counties & Regions (Answers)

71- A

72- C

73- C

74- D

75- B

76- B

77- A

78- B

79- D

80- C

81- A

82- B

83- D

84- D

85- C

86- C

87- A

88- B

89- A

90- C

Mountains

91- The annual rainfall here measures approximately 20 inches.

(A)- Lake Mountain (Victoria)

(B)- Mabla Mountains

(C)- Khentii Mountains

(D)- Cordillera de Talamanca

92- The tallest summit of this mountain is Mount Gongga.

(A)- Sulaiman Mountains

(B)- Blue Ridge Mountains

(C)- Hengduan Mountains

(D)- Wuyi Mountains

93- In the early 1980s, a deposit of gemstone-quality clinohumite was discovered in these mountains.

(A)- Long Range Mountains

(B)- Pamir Mountains

(C)- Crimean Mountains

(D)- Tatra Mountains

94- This place is also known as the Urgoma Mountains.

(A)- Jenny Jump Mountain

(B)- Mount Wilhelm

(C)- Bale Mountains

(D)- Mount Gilboa

95- This range is arguably the oldest geological feature on Earth, having its origin in the Proterozoic era.

(A)- Aravalli Range

(B)- Wasatch Range

(C)- Bear River Range

(D)- Verkhoyansk Range

96- Which one isn't in Utah?

(A)- Tokosha Mountains

(B)- Flat Top Mountain

(C)- Bald Mountain

(D)- Oquirrh Mountains

97- Which one is Mount Bigelow in?

(A)- Torngat Mountains

(B)- Jura Mountains

(C)- Santa Catalina Mountains

(D)- Lebombo Mountains

98- This place has over 7,402 species of flowering plants and 1,814 of non-flowering plants.

(A)- Harquahala Mountain

(B)- Western Ghats

(C)- Cho Oyu

(D)- Mount Robson

99- Francs Peak is located here.

(A)- Teton Range

(B)- Toba Kakar Range

(C)- Absaroka Range

(D)- Satpura Range

100- Which one has six peaks in the center of the Issaquah Alps.

(A)- Tiger Mountain

(B)- Mount St Helen's

(C)- Great Dividing Range

(D)- Mont Blanc

101- Which one is in Antarctica?

(A)- Mount Rumble

(B)- Blue Mountain Peak

(C)- Cerro Marahuaca

(D)- Crary Mountains

102- Geologically, this place belongs to the Alpide belt system that extends from southeastern Europe into Asia and is considered a border between the two continents.

(A)- Amerrisque Mountains

(B)- Mount Porte Crayon

(C)- Caucasus Mountains

(D)- Mount Pellegrino

103- This is the second tallest mountain in Japan.

(A)- Wedge Mountain

(B)- Mount Kita

(C)- Mount Zion

(D)- Goose Creek Mountains

104- The topographic prominence here is 4,665 ft.

(A)- Mount Parker (Hong Kong)

(B)- El Picacho

(C)- Nevado Tres Cruces

(D)- Xixiabangma Peak

105- Which one has been nicknamed the "Beast of Provence."

(A)- Mount Ventoux

(B)- Calapooya Mountains

(C)- Tacaná Volcano

(D)- Gannett Peak

106- This is an isolated mountain range in northern Colombia.

(A)- Pico Paraná

(B)- Sierra Nevada de Santa Marta

(C)- Bonanza Peak

(D)- Cheam Peak

107- This mountain is in north-eastern Corfu.

(A)- Mount Pantokrator

(B)- Hajar Mountains

(C)- Mount Sanford

(D)- Great Smoky Mountains

108- Which one is the highest mountain of the Saguenay-Lac Saint-Jean region?

(A)- Mount Narodnaya

(B)- Mount Valin

(C)- Östliche Karwendelspitze

(D)- Mount Nittany

109- The elevation here is 14,011 ft.

(A)- West Maui Mountains

(B)- Mount of the Holy Cross

(C)- Ko'olau Range

(D)- Aonach Beag

110- This is the second highest peak in Romania.

(A)- Wilsons Peak

(B)- Spicers Peak

(C)- Castle Peak

(D)- Negoiu Peak

Mountains (Answers)

91- B

92- C

93- B

94- C

95- A

96- A

97- C

98- B

99- C

100- A

101- D

102- C

103- B

104- C

105- A

106- B

107- A

108- B

109- B

110- D

United States

111 - This is the Grand Canyon State.

(A)- Nevada

(B)- New Mexico

(C)- Arizona

(D)- Colorado

112 - Mount Rushmore National Memorial is in this state.

(A)- Montana

(B)- South Dakota

(C)- Wyoming

(D)- North Dakota

113 - What was the first State in the United States?

(A)- Delaware

(B)- South Carolina

(C)- North Carolina

(D)- Arkansas

114 - This is known as the Empire State.

(A)- New Jersey

(B)- Virginia

(C)- West Virginia

(D)- New York

115 - On August 21, 1959, this became the 50th State.

(A)- Washington

(B)- Alaska

(C)- Hawai'i

(D)- Oklahoma

116 - Which state flag is the only non-rectangular flag of all the U.S. states?

(A)- New Hampshire

(B)- Ohio

(C)- Illinois

(D)- Missouri

117 - Which is the smallest state in the U.S.?

(A)- Rhode Island

(B)- Vermont

(C)- Maine

(D)- Kentucky

118 - On June 1, 1796, this became the 16th state in the U.S.

(A)- Alabama

(B)- Mississippi

(C)- Louisiana

(D)- Tennessee

119 - This state means "friends" in Caddo Indian.

(A)- Florida

(B)- Idaho

(C)- Texas

(D)- Indiana

120 - In 1803, the U.S. obtained this state as part of the Louisiana Purchase.

(A)- Iowa

(B)- Oregon

(C)- New Mexico

(D)- Georgia

121 - Which state isn't considered the Midwest?

(A)- Minnesota

(B)- Pennsylvania

(C)- Michigan

(D)- Wisconsin

122 - Currently in 2022, this state has a population of 2,954,832.

(A)- Kansas

(B)- North Dakota

(C)- Nebraska

(D)- Utah

123 - The nickname of this state is the "Bay State."

(A)- Connecticut

(B)- Massachusetts

(C)- California

(D)- Maryland

124 - As of 2022, how many states have no state income tax.

(A)- 7

(B)- 9

(C)- 12

(D)- 14

125 - Currently this state receives more snow per year than any other state.

(A)- Utah

(B)- Wisconsin

(C)- Vermont

(D)- Alaska

126- Currently in 2022, how many states don't trhave a population of a million people?

(A)- 2

(B)- 3

(C)- 5

(D)- 6

127- This state is the leading producer of pumpkins.

(A)- Nebraska

(B)- Iowa

(C)- Montana

(D)- Illinois

128- The 6th largest state in the nation, covering over 113,000 square miles is ....

(A)- Wyoming

(B)- Arizona

(C)- Oklahoma

(D)- Minnesota

129- What year did the Ohio legislature designate the Ohio Buckeye, *Aesculus glabra*, as Ohio's official state tree?

(A)- 1788

(B)- 1870

(C)- 1910

(D)- 1953

130- In 2020, this state generated around $7.7 billion in agricultural cash receipts.

(A)- Kentucky

(B)- Texas

(C)- Georgia

(D)- Washington

United States (Answers)

111- C

112- B

113- A

114- D

115- C

116- B

117- A

118- D

119- C

120- A

121- B

122- A

123- B

124- B

125- C

126- C

127- D

128- B

129- D

130- C

Forests

131- This place was established on July 1, 1908.

(A)- Chattahoochee-Oconee National Forest

(B)- Arapaho National Forest

(C)- Naz Perce National Forest

(D)- Caribou-Targhee National Forest

132- This forest is in Balochistan, Pakistan.

(A)- Ziarat Juniper Forest

(B)- Sherbrooke Forest

(C)- Rosh HaAyin Forest

(D)- Białowieża Forest

133- Approximately 8,000 acres of forest is designated as wilderness, with no roads or logging allowed.

(A)- Shawnee State Forest

(B)- Passa Quatro National Forest

(C)- Congo Rainforest

(D)- Brown Mountain Forest

134- In 2010, this forest was honored with its own quarter under the America the Beautiful Quarters program.

(A)- Morgan Hill State Forest

(B)- El Yunque National Forest

(C)- Brendan T. Byrne State Forest

(D)- Mount Hood National Forest

135- Which one was established on September 15, 1980?

(A)- Blackbird State Forest

(B)- Sa Nang Manora Forest Park

(C)- Tiger Bay State Forest

(D)- Rio Preto National Forest

136- This ecoregion covers an area of approximately 29,900 sq miles.

(A)- Tillamook State Forest

(B)- Sinaloan Dry Forests

(C)- Black Hills National Forest

(D)- Daintree Forest

137- This is the second largest man-made forest in southern Ontario.

(A)- Avondale Forest

(B)- Larose Forest

(C)- Toolangi State Forest

(D)- Kukrail Reserve Forest

138- Researchers estimate the extent of old growth in this forest is 18,900 acres.

(A)- Beartown State Forest

(B)- Karkloof Forest

(C)- Wielangta Forest

(D)- Los Padres National Forest

139- This forest has around 219 bird species and 79 mammal species.

(A)- English Lowlands Beech Forests

(B)- Kielder Forest

(C)- Six Rivers National Forest

(D)- North Central Rockies Forests

140- Which place has a total area of 4,031,999?

(A)- Amazon Rainforest

(B)- Beaverhead-Deerlodge National Forest

(C)- Newfoundland Highland Forests

(D)- Sandilands Provincial Forest

141- Rainfall averages 730-1200 mm per year here.

(A)- Valdivian Temperate Rainforest

(B)- Silkeborg Forests

(C)- Jalisco Dry Forests

(D)- Forest of Chaux

142- This place was established on October 13, 1936.

(A)- Dixon Memorial State Forest

(B)- Dainava Forest

(C)- Davy Crockett National Forest

(D)- Dhlinza Forest

143- This area has 10,836 acres.

(A)- Três Barras National Forest

(B)- Great Bear Rainforest

(C)- Bald Eagle State Forest

(D)- Northern Highland-American Legion State Forest

144- In 1907, this was created from a portion of forest reserve, which had been one of the first of its kind, designated in 1892.

(A)- Chugach National Forest

(B)- Eawy Forest

(C)- Mid-Continental Canadian Forests

(D)- Knobs State Forest

145- In 2021, this forest had 1.3 million visitors, marking the most ever for this location.

(A)- Alberta Mountain Forests

(B)- Restinga de Cabedelo National Forest

(C)- DuPont State Forest

(D)- Sinharaja Forest Reserve

Forests (Answers)

131- C

132- A

133- A

134- D

135- B

136- B

137- B

138- D

139- D

140- C

141- C

142- C

143- A

144- A

145- C

Cities

146- This city doesn't have an airport, so people must go to a town called Alajuela.

(A)- Scarborough, Trinidad, and Tobago

(B)- Brasília, Brasil

(C)- Venice, Italy

(D)- San José, Costa Rica

147- Which city hosted the 1976 Summer Olympics?

(A)- Montreal, Canada

(B)- Barcelona, Spain

(C)- Athens, Greece

(D)- Munich, West Germany

148- With a population of 242,524 this is the largest city of Bosnia and Herzegovina.

(A)- Sarajevo

(B)- Zenica

(C)- Bijeljina

(D)- Mostar

149- This city is the host of the self-proclaimed "World's Oldest Rodeo."

(A)- Paradise Valley, Arizona

(B)- Tombstone, Arizona

(C)- Oro Valley, Arizona

(D)- Prescott, Arizona

150- Since 2001, Taizhou, Jiangsu is the sister city with ....

(A)- Montevideo, Uruguay

(B)- Kotka, Finland

(C)- Luxor, Egypt

(D)- Banff, Alberta

151- The Anakeesta theme park is in this city.

(A)- Gatlinburg, Tennessee

(B)- Wiesbaden, Germany

(C)- Palermo, Italy

(D)- Kharkiv, Ukraine

152- This city is known as the "Summer Capital of the Philippines."

(A)- Parañaque

(B)- Baguio

(C)- Iligan

(D)- Zamboanga

153- Which one is also known as Cape Comorin.

(A)- Kanyakumari, India

(B)- Taichung City, Taiwan

(C)- Algiers, Algeria

(D)- Garden City, Utah

154- The headquarters for Eurac Research is here.

(A)- Tijuana, Mexico

(B)- Chelsea, London

(C)- Amsterdam, Netherlands

(D)- Bolzano, Italy

155- This city is known for being the only place where the rare Larimar stone can be found.

(A)- Barahona, Dominican Republic

(B)- Lewiston, Idaho

(C)- Gjilan, Kosovo

(D)- Dakar, Senegal

156- In 2002, this city was awarded the UNESCO Cities for Peace Prize for addressing the challenges of rapid urbanization.

(A)- Bern, Switzerland

(B)- Shillong, India

(C)- Bahir Dar, Ethiopia

(D)- Punta Gorda, Florida

157- This city has the world's largest cashew tree.

(A)- Bellevue, Washington

(B)- Natal, Rio Grande do Norte

(C)- Reyjavik, Iceland

(D)- Essaouira, Morocco

158- Mount Baldhead is across from this city.

(A)- Stirling, Scotland

(B)- Dubai, United Arab Emirates

(C)- Saugatuck, Michigan

(D)- Choloma, Honduras

159- Which city is in Trinidad and Tobago?

(A)- Bosaso

(B)- Piarco

(C)- Novosibirsk

(D)- Ooty

160- In 2019, this city was ranked in the top 10 most livable cities according to Mercer.

(A)- Basel, Switzerland

(B)- Jūrmala, Latvia

(C)- Great Falls, Montana

(D)- Picton, New Zealand

161- Park of the Pomeranian Dukes is here.

(A)- Koszalin, Poland

(B)- Giza, Egypt

(C)- Thunder Bay, Ontario

(D)- Plymouth, Massachusetts

162- Where is the University of Northern Colorado located?

(A)- Greeley, Colorado

(B)- Crested Butte, Colorado

(C)- Glenwood Springs, Colorado

(D)- Telluride, Colorado

163- The Global Destination Sustainability Index has named this city the world's most sustainable destination every year since 2016.

(A)- Selfoss, Iceland

(B)- Innsbruck, Austria

(C)- Winnemucca, Nevada

(D-) Gothenburg, Sweden

164- The 2022 metro area population for this place is 2.3 million.

(A)- Chamonix, France

(B)- Maracaibo, Venezuela

(C)- Morón, Cuba

(D)- Grass Valley, California

165- In 1988, the city historic center and the adjacent mines were proclaimed a World Heritage Site by UNESCO.

(A)- Roskilde, Denmark

(B)- Cork, Ireland

(C)- Győr, Hungary

(D)- Guanajuato, Mexico

166- In 1951, construction for the Great Hall of the People was started here.

(A)- Plzeň, Czech Republic

(B)- Temecula, California

(C)- Rakvere, Estonia

(D)- Chongqing, China

167- This city is known as the "Queen City of the Kootenays."

(A)- Stone Town, Tanzania

(B)- Cape May, New Jersey

(C)- Nelson, British Columbia

(D)- Cuenca, Ecuador

168- The Sugar Loaf bluff is located here.

(A)- Lancaster, Pennsylvania

(B)- Winona, Minnesota

(C)- Crazy Horse, South Dakota

(D)- Stowe, Vermont

169- On May 1, 2018, Fins Medical University was established here.

(A)- Herceg Novi, Montenegro

(B)- Kutaisi, Georgia

(C)- Fort Portal, Uganda

(D)- Marseille, France

170- The triumphal arch Hadrian's Gate is in this city.

(A)- Antalya, Turkey

(B)- Bucharest, Romania

(C)- Koper, Slovenia

(D)- Conakry, Guinea

Cities (Answers)

146- D

147- A

148- A

149- D

150- B

151- A

152- B

153- A

154- D

155- A

156- C

157- B

158- C

159- B

160- A

161- A

162- A

163- D

164- B

165- D

166- D

167- C

168- B

169- C

170- A

Mixed Part 1

171- Which place is in the Philippines?

(A)- Quezon Protected Landscape

(B)- Mombasa Marine National Park and Reserve

(C)- Gulmarg Wildlife Sanctuary

(D)- Haikou Volcanic Cluster Global Geopark

172- This place has over 650 species of butterflies, 330 species of birds, and 49 species of mammals.

(A)- Sokhondo Nature Reserve

(B)- Shantar Islands National Park

(C)- Gola Rainforest National Park

(D)- Wollemi National Park

173- The core of this area was declared a natural reserve on June 30, 1925.

(A)- Kirkjubæjarklaustur

(B)- Krasnoyarsk Pillars

(C)- Kinglake National Park

(D)- Kolmården Wildlife Park

174- Which one is also known as Crocodile Island?

(A)- Ascension Island

(B)- Rock Island State Park

(C)- Beltrami Island State Forest

(D)- Central Island

175- Moss Glen Falls is in this area.

(A)- Waterfall Remanso

(B)- Granville Gulf Reservation

(C)- Ikogosi Warm Springs

(D)- Munyon Island

176- The Alcock memorial is on the slopes of ....

(A)- Newberry National Volcanic Monument

(B)- Bruce Peninsula

(C)- Topčider

(D)- Carrickgollogan

177- This place is 254,980 acres.

(A)- Great Otway National Park

(B)- Cumberland Mountain State Park

(C)- Botaniska trädgården

(D)- Hawai'i Tropical Botanic Garden

178- Eldred Rock is located by this place.

(A)- Haines Borough, Alaska

(B)- Escanaba, Michigan

(C)- Terre Haute, Indiana

(D)- Rindge, New Hampshire

179- On July 25, 1996, this place was added to the U.S. National Register of Historic Places.

(A)- Bryce Canyon National Park

(B)- Hocking Hills State Park

(C)- Table Mountain National Park

(D)- Wadsworth Falls State Park

180- From June to October, this place is closed every year throughout the monsoon season.

(A)- Gir National Park

(B)- Ueckermünde Heath

(C)- Great North Woods

(D)- Monarch Butterfly Biosphere Reserve

181- There are 73 breeding species of birds here.

(A)- Bai Tho Mountain

(B)- Great Cypress Swamp

(C)- State Forest State Park

(D)- Niagara Glen Nature Reserve

182- Which one is in Tooele County?

(A)- New Hance Trail

(B)- Lake Louise

(C)- Subterranean River

(D)- Bonneville Salt Flats

183- Which place is in the Squamish-Lillooet regional district?

(A)- Alice Springs, Australia

(B)- Whistler, British Columbia

(C)- Tarawa, Kiribati

(D)- Northeast Region, Brasil

184- The shore length here is 4,300 miles.

(A)- Saint Martin

(B)- Blue Lagoon

(C)- Caspian Sea

(D)- Singer Island

185- The managing authorities for this location is the Queensland Parks and Wildlife Service.

(A)- Fiery Gizzard Trail

(B)- Andaman Islands

(C)- Springbrook National Park

(D)- Pigeon Valley

186- This place has 220 bird species and 56 mammal species.

(A)- Eastern Great Lakes Lowland Forests

(B)- Backbone State Park

(C)- Miombo Woodlands

(D)- Joseph E. Ibberson Conservation Area

187- About 439 million people live here.

(A)- Europe

(B)- Antarctica

(C)- Africa

(D)- South America

188- Which one features the world's tallest icefall at 3,600 ft?

(A)- Jelaiah

(B)- Hailuogou

(C)- Yakutsk

(D)- Saana

189- This location was designated a UNESCO World Heritage Site in 2014.

(A)- Batteaux Bay

(B)- Anahim Volcanic Belt

(C)- The Grand Canal

(D)- Ohio Bush Creek

190- Most of this place falls within the Swiss district of Maloja in the canton of the Grisons.

(A)- Sundarbans

(B)- Garampani Wildlife Sanctuary

(C)- Val Bregaglia

(D)- Laurentian Mixed Forest Province

191- On November 8, 2005, this place was incorporated.

(A)- Star Valley Ranch, Wyoming

(B)- Spanish Town, British Virgin Islands

(C)- Caledon, South Africa

(D)- Monowi, Nebraska

192- This place was established in 1955.

(A)- El Rey Archaeological Site

(B)- Tadoba Andhari Tiger Reserve

(C)- Cuyahoga Valley National Park

(D)- Balbirnie Stone Circle

193- One of the world's three largest oceanic oxygen minimum zones (OMZ) is here.

(A)- River Great Ouse

(B)- African Great Lakes

(C)- Shirogane Blue Pond

(D)- Arabian Sea

194- Since February 23, 1965, Mobile, Alabama has been the sister with ....

(A)- Elche

(B)- Córdoba

(C)- Zaragoza

(D)- Málaga

195- Its water capacity is approximately 273 million cubic meters.

(A)- Dead Sea

(B)- Morning Glory Pool

(C)- High Island Reservoir

(D)- Yucatán Peninsula

196- According to the 2011 census, this place had a population of 364 people.

(A)- Sveti Stefan

(B)- Neve Zohar

(C)- Ramla Bay

(D)- Playa Maderas

197- This place was founded on May 15, 1882.

(A)- St Asaph

(B)- Davyd-Haradok

(C)- Vaduz, Liechtenstein

(D)- Ensenada, Baja California

198- Which place is in Fitzroy County?

(A)- Montmorency Falls

(B)- Cumberland Caverns

(C)- Coffs Harbour

(D)- Seneca Rocks

199- This place has over 4,700 acres.

(A)- Volcán de Fuego

(B)- Hoover Reservoir Park

(C)- Saholan Cave

(D)- The Flower Fields

200- In 1879, this place received Municipal status.

(A)- Oaxaca City

(B)- Hato Mayor del Rey

(C)- Fraser Valley

(D)- Aberystwyth

Mixed Part 1 (Answers)

171- A

172- C

173- B

174- D

175- B

176- D

177- A

178- A

179- D

180- A

181- B

182- D

183- B

184- C

185- C

186- A

187- D

188- B

189- C

190- C

191- A

192- B

193- D

194- D

195- C

196- A

197- D

198- C

199- B

200- A

Rivers

201- This is the second largest river in Central America and the longest in Honduras.

(A)- Loutre River

(B)- Tapi River

(C)- Sauble River

(D)- Patuca River

202- Which one is the longest river in Europe?

(A)- Barak River

(B)- Ob River

(C)- Cheat River

(D)- Volga River

203- Which river is in South Central Alaska?

(A)- Yentna River

(B)- Farmington River

(C)- Kintrishi River

(D)- Saloum River

204- The length of this river is 3,030 miles.

(A)- Bolshaya Ussurka

(B)- Paranoá River

(C)- Matawin River (Quebec)

(D)- Clearwater River

205- This is the largest river in Guyana.

(A)- Eleven Point River

(B)- Coco River

(C)- Essequibo River

(D)- Congo River

206- This is a major river in Siberia.

(A)- Angara River

(B)- Yellow River

(C)- Yenisei River

(D)- Paraná River

207- This river flows through Gangwon and Gyeonggi Provinces.

(A)- Ucayali River

(B)- Zambezi River

(C)- Murrumbidgee River

(D)- Hantan River

208- This river rises in Colombia and flows eastward through Brasil to join the Amazon River.

(A)- Arno River

(B)- Yuna River

(C)- Japurá River

(D)- Columbia River

209- This river is a continuation of the western branch of the Balonne River.

(A)- Nile River

(B)- Culgoa River

(C)- Missouri River

(D)- River Wye

210- More than 70% of Delhi's water supply is from this river.

(A)- Ourthe River

(B)- Yamuna River

(C)- Dnipro River

(D)- Rhine River

211- This river is commonly referred to as the Pagsanjan River.

(A)- Tapajós River

(B)- Colorado River

(C)- Bumbungan River

(D)- Soča River

212- There are four headworks on this river Marala, Khanki, Qadirabad, and Trimmu Barrage.

(A)- Chenab River

(B)- Saint Lawrence River

(C)- Seomjin River

(D)- Dnieper River

213- Which river is in Canada?

(A)- Snake River

(B)- Usumacinta River

(C)- Minjiang River

(D)- Coppermine River

214- On May 5, 1819, the first European to discover this watercourse was explorer Charles Throsby.

(A)- Klarälven River

(B)- River Nene

(C)- Vinne River

(D)- Abercrombie River

215- The total drainage area for this river is 321,500 sq miles.

(A)- Bui River

(B)- Liard River

(C)- Flint River

(D)- Yukon River

216- This is the tenth longest river in Italy.

(A)- Reno River

(B)- Martha Brae River

(C)- Irtysh River

(D)- Tefé River

217- Which river isn't in Mexico?

(A)- Jamapa River

(B)- Yaqui River

(C)- Chavón River

(D)- Nazas River

218- This is a tributary to the Ume River.

(A)- Rima River

(B)- Vindel River

(C)- Amazon River

(D)- Tennessee River

219- This is the most polluted river in Europe.

(A)- Abulug River

(B)- Sundays River

(C)- Sarno River

(D)- Adda River

220- This river is known to contain 49 species of zooplankton.

(A)- Ogunpa River

(B)- Mississippi River

(C)- Ohio River

(D)- Thames River

Rivers (Answers)

201- D

202- D

203- A

204- B

205- C

206- A

207- D

208- C

209- B

210- B

211- C

212- A

213- D

214- D

215- D

216- A

217- C

218- B

219- C

220- A

Deserts

221 - The Red Desert is in ....

(A)- Arizona

(B)- Wyoming

(C)- California

(D)- Texas

222- Te Onetapu, is commonly known as the ....

(A)- Rangipo Desert

(B)- Strzelecki Desert

(C)- Judaean Desert

(D)- Nubian Desert

223- This is the hottest desert in both Mexico and the United States.

(A)- Chihuahuan Desert

(B)- Grand Bara Desert

(C)- Sonoran Desert

(D)- Ordos Desert

224- The largest desert in the world is ....

(A)- Artic Desert

(B)- Great Sandy Desert

(C)- Antarctic Desert

(D)- Syrian Desert

225- La Guajira Desert is in ....

(A)- Chile and Peru

(B)- Brasil and Bolivia

(C)- Paraguay and Uruguay

(D)- Colombia and Venezuela

226 - This desert covers much of Botswana and parts of Namibia and South Africa.

(A)- Sahara Desert

(B)- Kalahari Desert

(C)- Lompoul Desert

(D)- Sinai Desert

227 - Which one isn't located in Europe?

(A)- Monegros Desert

(B)- Thompson Plateau

(C)- Oltenian Sahara

(D)- Highlands of Iceland

228- This place is also called the "Empty Quarter."

(A)- Rub' al Khali

(B)- Dungeness

(C)- Jalapão

(D)- Death Valley

229- Which desert is in China?

(A)- Mojave Desert

(B)- Patagonian Desert

(C)- Taklamakan Desert

(D)- Nyiri Desert

230 - The Great Victoria Desert is the largest in ....

(A)- Saudi Arabia

(B)- Canada

(C)- Australia

(D)- Argentina

231- This is a small desert close to the South Pole.

(A)- Meyer Desert

(B)- Tabernas Desert

(C)- Błędów Desert

(D)- Karoo Desert

232 - This is a desert and semidesert region of southern Israel.

(A)- Sharqiya Sands

(B)- Tanezrouft

(C)- El Djouf

(D)- Negev

233- This desert is also known as the "Great Indian Desert."

(A)- Dasht-e Margo

(B)- Thar Desert

(C)- Desert of Wales

(D)- Syrian Desert

234 - This is a cold desert in Pakistan.

(A)- Gurbantünggüt Desert

(B)- Great Basin Desert

(C)- Karakum Desert

(D)- Katpana Desert

235- How many separate desert regions does Arizona have?

(A)- 3

(B)- 4

(C)- 5

(D)- 6

Deserts (Answers)

221- B

222- A

223- C

224- C

225- D

226- B

227- B

228- A

229- C

230- C

231- A

232- D

233- B

234- D

235- B

Lakes

236- The water volume here is 53,535,000 acre-ft.

(A)- Frying Pan Lake

(B)- Waterton Lake

(C)- Lake Nojiri

(D)- Khyargas Lake

237- This lake was one of the largest lakes in the world in the 1820s.

(A)- Lake Chad

(B)- Lake Arpi

(C)- Todd Lake

(D)- Lake Akan

238- In 1995, annual fish production here was about 7,000 tons, 100 tons of shrimp and 1.5 million crayfish.

(A)- Hulun Lake

(B)- Lake Claire (Alberta)

(C)- Lake Pleshcheyevo

(D)- Lake Francis (Murphy Dam)

239- The image of this lake was on the reverse side of the 1969 and 1979 issues of the Canadian twenty-dollar bill.

(A)- Lake Prespa

(B)- Lake Koocanusa

(C)- Gaładuś Lake

(D)- Moraine Lake

240- Sometimes this lake is home to one of the world's largest populations of lesser flamingos.

(A)- Rainy Lake

(B)- Cami Lake

(C)- Lake Bogoria

(D)- Lake Tahoe

241- This is one of the largest hypersaline lakes in the world.

(A)- Viedma Lake

(B)- Sarez Lake

(C)- Lake Tuz

(D)- Lake Albert (Africa)

242- This lake was given its present name in 1865.

(A)- Lake Sevan

(B)- Lake Garda

(C)- Lake Hornavan

(D)- Lake Carasaljo

243- Which one is home to 305 bird species, 42 species of mammals, and over 590 insect species?

(A)- Great Slave Lake

(B)- Torch Lake

(C)- Torey Lakes

(D)- Great Lakes

244- This lake is the second largest lake in Italy and the largest in southern Switzerland.

(A)- Lake Bolsena

(B)- Lachuá Lake

(C)- Lake Maggiore

(D)- Lake Titicaca

245- This lake is known as the only place in the world where mail jumping is practiced.

(A)- Lake Mashū

(B)- Geneva Lake

(C)- Albigna Lake

(D)- Moosehead Lake

246- Which lake is in the Raposa Serra do Sol indigenous territory?

(A)- Lake Caracaranã

(B)- Lake Ruhondo

(C)- Lake Kournas

(D)- Lake Baikal

247- At over 1,300 ft deep, this is the fifth deepest lake in Europe.

(A)- Lake Alpsee

(B)- Lake Jocassee

(C)- Lake Toba

(D)- Lake Como

248- This lake was built in 1928.

(A)- Beech Hill Lake

(B)- Guajataca Lake

(C)- Agency Lake

(D)- Patoka Lake

249- In 2012, Taylor Odom caught a 10.64-pound bass that broke lake records here.

(A)- Tony Grove Lake

(B)- Green River Lake

(C)- Sunburst Lake

(D)- Okatibbee Lake

250- The water volume of this lake is 179,880 acre-ft.

(A)- Eagle Mountain Lake

(B)- Patagonia Lake

(C)- Lake Balkhash

(D)- Lake Carina Forest Preserve Pond

251- This lake holds the state record for producing the largest muskie ever caught. In 2000, Jerrold Seibert's catch was 54" long and weighed in at 44 pounds.

(A)- Lake Roland (Maryland)

(B)- Crystal Palace Park Lake

(C)- Salt Fork Lake

(D)- Lake Tanganyika

252- The surface area of this lake is 1,290 sq miles.

(A)- General Carrera Lake

(B)- Dal Lake

(C)- Uvs Lake

(D)- Redfish Lake

253- This is the smallest of the Fuji Five Lakes in terms of surface area, and third deepest, with a maximum water depth of 50 ft.

(A)- Lake Shōji

(B)- Lake Orta

(C)- Lake Pancharevo

(D)- Heaven Lake

254- This is the largest freshwater lake in Florida.

(A)- Lake Ewauna

(B)- Lake Shikotsu

(C)- Lake San Cristobal

(D)- Lake Okeechobee

255- The city of Twin Falls purchased this lake in 1969.

(A)- Lake Nockamixon

(B)- New Melones Lake

(C)- Dierkes Lake

(D)- Lake Travis

Lakes (Answers)

236- D

237- A

238- A

239- D

240- C

241- C

242- D

243- C

244- C

245- B

246- A

247- D

248- B

249- D

250- A

251- C

252- C

253- A

254- D

255- C

Countries

256- How many countries are on the African continent?

(A)- 35

(B)- 54

(C)- 69

(D)- 88

257- Burma is now known as ....

(A)- Sri Lanka

(B)- Bhutan

(C)- Myanmar

(D)- Holy See

258- Which place was formerly named Swaziland?

(A)- Cabo Verde

(B)- Armenia

(C)- Marshall Islands

(D)- Eswatini

259- This is an island country in the Polynesian subregion of Oceania.

(A)- Tuvalu

(B)- Philippines

(C)- Moldova

(D)- Suriname

260- The 2022 estimate nominal GDP total for this country is $47.745 billion.

(A)- Norway

(B)- Serbia

(C)- Yemen

(D)- Jordan

261- They have the world's 23rd most powerful passport as of 2022 and offer citizenship by investment program.

(A)- Sao Tome and Principle

(B)- United States of America

(C)- Antigua and Barbuda

(D)- El Salvador

262- Which one is the world's second-largest island country?

(A)- Madagascar

(B)- South Sudan

(C)- North Korea

(D)- Portugal

263- Which one has an area of 55,300 square miles?

(A)- Tajikistan

(B)- Micronesia

(C)- Seychelles

(D)- Algeria

264- This is one of Europe's smallest countries currently ranking 167th in size of the 194 independent countries in the world.

(A)- Luxembourg

(B)- Nauru

(C)- Burkina Faso

(D)- Kyrgyzstan

265- Scientists have identified 306 species of birds within this country's borders.

(A)- United Kingdom

(B)- Italy

(C)- Dominican Republic

(D)- Slovenia

266- This place is known as the "Frying Pan of the World."

(A)- Kuwait

(B)- Niger

(C)- Haiti

(D)- Mozambique

267- The flowers here are one of the biggest tourist attractions.

(A)- Saint Kitts and Nevis

(B)- Afghanistan

(C)- Netherlands

(D)- Comoros

268- This country has white mud found in the Milky Way Lagoon on Koror Island. People consider it a natural spa.

(A)- Palau

(B)- Kirbati

(C)- San Marino

(D)- Mauritania

269- This place has 5 UNESCO world heritage sites, 2 national parks and 9 natural reserves.

(A)- Uzbekistan

(B)- Saudi Arabia

(C)- Palestine State

(D)- Japan

270- The town of Ureka in this area is one of the wettest in the world.

(A)- Indonesia

(B)- Solomon Islands

(C)- Canada

(D)- Equatorial Guinea

271- The only country in the world that has Catalan as its only official language.

(A)- Andorra

(B)- United Arab Emirates

(C)- Guinea-Bissau

(D)- Turkmenistan

272- As of 2022, the population here is 168,515, 636.

(A)- Bangladesh

(B)- Czech Republic

(C)- Laos

(D)- Belize

273- This is the only country in the world that is entirely above 1,000m (3,281 ft), higher than any other country.

(A)- Azerbaijan

(B)- Côte d'Ivoire

(C)- Lesotho

(D)- Timor-Leste

274- The world's most accessible volcano (Mount Yasur) is found here.

(A)- Bahrain

(B)- Vanuatu

(C)- Colombia

(D)- Thailand

275- This is the second most mountainous country in the world.

(A)- North Macedonia

(B)- Saint Vincent and the Grenadines

(C)- Maldives

(D)- Pakistan

276- On October 10, 1970, this place gained independence.

(A)- China

(B)- Fiji

(C)- Central African Republic

(D)- Hungary

277- This place is considered the birthplace of rum.

(A)- Barbados

(B)- France

(C)- Croatia

(D)- Denmark

278- This is one of the sunniest places in the world.

(A)- Honduras

(B)- Germany

(C)- Nicaragua

(D)- Greece

279- Around 20% of all the trees in the world are here.

(A)- Brasil

(B)- Australia

(C)- Russia

(D)- Mexico

280- This country had a 3.64/10 score in the 2019 Forest Landscape Integrity Index, ranking it 144th globally out of 172 countries.

(A)- Iraq

(B)- Egypt

(C)- Nepal

(D)- Syria

Countries (Answers)

256- B

257- C

258- D

259- A

260- D

261- C

262- A

263- A

264- A

265- C

266- B

267- C

268- A

269- A

270- D

271- A

272- A

273- C

274- B

275- A

276- B

277- A

278- D

279- C

280- D

Provinces

281- Which province isn't in the Philippines?

(A)- Cebu

(B)- Quezon

(C)- Saba

(D)- Masbate

282- How many provinces in Italy?

(A)- 82

(B)- 94

(C)- 107

(D)- 221

283- Which province in Canada didn't enter the Confederation on July 1, 1867?

(A)- Manitoba

(B)- Nova Scotia

(C)- Ontario

(D)- Quebec

284- In the latter half of the Qing dynasty (1644-1912), there were how many Qing provinces?

(A)- 7

(B)- 18

(C)- 24

(D)- 33

285- Afghanistan is divided into how many provinces?

(A)- 15

(B)- 27

(C)- 34

(D)- 46

286- This province in Cuba was founded in 1879.

(A)- Holguin

(B)- Santiago de Cuba

(C)- La Habana

(D)- Pinar del Rio

287- As of 2019, this province had a population of 1,248,415.

(A)- Sơn La

(B)- Yên Bái

(C)- Hà Tĩnh

(D)- Kon Tum

288- This is the most populous province in the Netherlands.

(A)- Zeeland

(B)- Friesland

(C)- South Holland

(D)- Flevoland

289- Which one has been a province since October 16, 2001?

(A)- Santo Domingo

(B)- Kongo Central

(C)- Guayas

(D)- Northern Cape

290- This is an abolished province.

(A)- Herat Province

(B)- Province of Aosta

(C)- Prince Edward Island

(D)- Overijssel

291- Which place isn't a province?

(A)- Badakshan

(B)- Alberta

(C)- Zamora

(D)- Ozark

292- Xinjiang spans over ....

(A)- 60,000 sq miles

(B)- 80,000 sq miles

(C)- 474,300 Sq miles

(D)- 625,000 sq miles

293- This is an Algerian Province created in 2019.

(A)- Santa Cruz Province

(B)- El Menia Province

(C)- Salavan Province

(D)- Estuaire Province

294- This is the southernmost province of Burundi.

(A)- Makamba

(B)- Wele-Nzas

(C)- Koh Kong

(D)- Cartago

295- The Van Don International Airport is in this province.

(A)- Saskatchewan

(B)- Utrecht

(C)- Sar-e Pol

(D)- Quảng Ninh

296- This is the smallest province in Zambia.

(A)- Luapula Province

(B)- Muchinga Province

(C)- Lusaka Province

(D)- Copperbelt Province

297- The only province in Peru that doesn't belong to any of the 25 regions is ....

(A)- Monte Plata Province

(B)- Sanma Province

(C)- Lima Province

(D)- Uva Province

298- Currently, this province has 9 districts.

(A)- Matabeleland North

(B)- Mashonaland East

(C)- Matabeleland South

(D)- Mashonaland West

299- This province was created in 1993 out of part of the Tehran Province.

(A)- Qazvin Province

(B)- Punjab Province

(C)- Shahumyan Province

(D)- Manica Province

300- On July 14, 1950, this place was legally re-established.

(A)- West Java

(B)- North Sumatra

(C)- Central Java

(D)- East Java

Provinces (Answers)

281- C

282- C

283- A

284- B

285- C

286- D

287- A

288- C

289- A

290- B

291- D

292- D

293- B

294- A

295- D

296- C

297- C

298- B

299- A

300- A

Indian Reservations & Tribal Homelands

301- This reservation in Washington currently consists of 2,825,000 acres (4,410 sq miles).

(A)- Colville Indian Reservation

(B)- Coushatta Indian Reservation

(C)- Cocopah Indian Reservation

(D)- Coquille Indian Reservation

302- The Penobscot Indian Island Reservation is in ....

(A)- Maine

(B)- Ohio

(C)- Hawai'i

(D)- New Mexico

303- How many Indian Reservations are in the United States?

(A)- 165

(B)- 237

(C)- 326

(D)- 441

304- The Allegany Indian Reservation in New York had this population in 2010 ....

(A)- 2,185

(B)- 6,490

(C)- 8,090

(D)- 10,008

305- The Fort Mojave Indian Reservation are federally recognized in these places.

(A)- Kansas, Missouri, and Nebraska

(B)- Minnesota, Wisconsin, and Iowa

(C)- Arizona, California, and Nevada

(D)- Idaho, Utah, and Montana

306- This Indian Reservation is in Michigan.

(A)- Ontonagon Indian Reservation

(B)- Kaibab Indian Reservation

(C)- Grand Portage Indian Reservation

(D)- Red Lake Indian Reservation

307- Which Indian Reservation isn't in Arizona?

(A)- San Carlos Reservation

(B)- Mesa Grande Reservation

(C)- Maricopa Ak Chin Indian Reservation

(D)- Salt River Reservation

308- They opened a casino on October 12, 1996.

(A)- Keweenaw Bay Indian Community

(B)- Chickasaw Nation

(C)- Mohegan Tribe

(D)- San Manuel Band of Mission Indians

309- Standing Rock Indian Reservation lies across the border of ....

(A)- North Carolina & South Carolina

(B)- Arizona & California

(C)- North Dakota & South Dakota

(D)- Washington & Oregon

310- As of the 2020 federal census, this reservation population was 4,526.

(A)- Omaha Reservation

(B)- Gila River Indian Reservation

(C)- Brighton Seminole Indian Reservation

(D)- Northern Cheyenne Indian Reservation

311- Fort Belknap Indian Reservation is shared by two Native American tribes.

(A)- Gros Ventre and Nakota

(B)- Sac and Meskwaki (Fox)

(C)- Cheyenne and Arapaho Tribes

(D)- Yurok and Tolowa

312- This is a state-recognized tribe in Georgia.

(A)- Chickahominy people

(B)- Nipmuc Nation

(C)- MOWA Band of Choctaw Indians

(D)- Lower Muskogee Creek Tribe

313- This tribe received official recognition in 1987.

(A)- Minnesota Chippewa Tribe

(B)- Aroostook Band of Micmacs

(C)- Pit River Tribe

(D)- Wampanoag Tribe of Gay Head

314- As of 2017, this Oklahoma tribe's economic impact is over $145 million dollars.

(A)- Wyandotte Nation

(B)- Cherokee Nation

(C)- Ponca Tribe of Indians of Oklahoma

(D)- Absentee Shawnee Tribe of Indians

315- Ysleta del Sure Pueblo is a Puebloan Native American tribal entity in the Ysleta section of ....

(A)- Sierra Vista, Arizona

(B)- Niobrara, Nebraska

(C)- El Paso, Texas

(D)- Tesuque, New Mexico

316- In October 2016, under the *Nevada Native Nations Land Act*, they were one of six federally recognized tribes in Nevada to have additional lands put into trust for their reservations.

(A)- Duckwater Shoshone Tribe

(B)- Tonto Apache

(C)- Narragansett people

(D)- Shoalwater Bay Tribe

317- Lower Sioux Indian Reservation is also known as ....

(A)- Rocky Boy's Indian Reservation

(B)- Mdewakanton Tribal Reservation

(C)- Umatilla Indian Reservation

(D)- Winnemucca Indian Colony

318- This reservation was established in 1913 and is 12,573 acres, with 10,098 acres of trust lands.

(A)- Roaring Creek Rancheria

(B)- Summit Lake Indian Reservation

(C)- Cold Springs Rancheria

(D)- Turtle Mountain Indian Reservation

319- This is a state-recognized tribe and nonprofit organization in North Carolina.

(A)- Haliwa-Saponi

(B)- Shinnecock Reservation

(C)- Qualla Boundary

(D)- Yerington Colony

320- This tribe is one of only two Virginia Indian tribes in the Commonwealth of Virginia that owns reservation land.

(A)- Lakota people

(B)- Cahto

(C)- Pascua Yaqui Tribe

(D)- Mattaponi

Indian Reservations & Tribal Homelands (Answers)

301- A

302- A

303- C

304- B

305- C

306- A

307- B

308- C

309- C

310- A

311- A

312- D

313- D

314- D

315- C

316- A

317- B

318- B

319- A

320- D

Botanical Gardens

321- One of the largest botanical gardens in Latin America is ....

(A)- Ljubljana Botanical Garden

(B)- Andromeda Botanic Gardens

(C)- Lancetilla Botanical Garden

(D)- Atatürk Arboretum

322- Where is Wagga Wagga Botanic Gardens located?

(A)- Bayan, Kuwait

(B)- Turvey Park, New South Wales

(C)- Zhengzhou, China

(D)- Tampere, Finland

323- This garden opened in 1958.

(A)- Trujillo Botanical Garden

(B)- Dominica Botanical Gardens

(C)- Atagawa Tropical & Alligator Garden

(D)- Agder Natural History Museum and Botanical Garden

324- This garden was opened to the public on December 8, 2002.

(A)- Botanical Garden of Merida

(B)- Nong Nooch Tropical Garden

(C)- Parque Municipal Summit

(D)- Taipei Botanical Garden

325- Established in 1638, this is one of the world's oldest botanical gardens.

(A)- Akureyri Botanical Garden

(B)- Jardín Botánico Nacional de Cuba

(C)- Hortus Botanicus

(D)- Tallinn Botanic Garden

326- This place reopened in 1995 only to be destroyed by Hurricane Marilyn three months later.

(A)- Ladew Topiary Gardens

(B)- Magens Bay Arboretum

(C)- Kalopa State Recreation Area

(D)- Blithewold Mansion, Gardens and Arboretum

327- This botanical garden has 4,500 flowers and 139 recorded bird species.

(A)- Kirstenbosch National Botanical Garden

(B)- San Juan Botanical Garden

(C)- United States Botanic Garden

(D)- Botanical Garden of Medellin

328- As many as 16,000 plant species can be seen outdoors as well as 4,000 species in the greenhouses.

(A)- Gothenburg Botanical Garden

(B)- Jardín Botánico La Carolina

(C)- Eram Garden

(D)- Jardín Botánico del Plan de la Laguna

329- Botanical Garden of the University of Vienna currently has gardens containing more than _____ species of plants.

(A)- 4,600

(B)- 7,100

(C)- 8,200

(D)- 11,500

330- Which botanic garden is operated by the University of Costa Rica?

(A)- Adelaide Botanic Garden

(B)- Lankester Botanical Garden

(C)- Artic-Alpine Botanical Garden

(D)- Cluj-Napoca Botanical Garden

331- This is one of three gardens, and the only tropical garden, to be honored as a UNESCO World Heritage Site.

(A)- Yerevan Botanical Gardens

(B)- Aburi Botanical Gardens

(C)- Thurston Gardens

(D)- Singapore Botanical Gardens

332- On June 30, 1806, the first trees were planted for the "Chemist's garden" and "botanical garden" here.

(A)- Glenbrook Native Plant Reserve

(B)- Malacca Botanical Garden

(C)- Gorky Park (Taganrog)

(D)- Queen Elizabeth II Botanic Park

333- This botanical garden is 406.4 acres.

(A)- Botanical Garden of São Paulo

(B)- Jardin des Serres d'Auteuil

(C)- Conservatory of Flowers

(D)- Brooklyn Botanic Garden

334- There are 485 rare and endangered species in care at this garden.

(A)- Bogotá Botanical Garden

(B)- Jardin Exotique de Monaco

(C)- Trsteno Arboretum

(D)- Desert Botanical Garden

335- In 2022, this was the first botanical garden outside of the United States to win the "Gardens of Excellence" Award from the American Public Garden Association.

(A)- Montreal Botanical Garden

(B)- St. Lucia Botanical Gardens

(C)- Vallarta Botanical Garden

(D)- Guyana Botanical Gardens

336- With more than 6.6 million specimens, its herbarium is the second largest in North America.

(A)- San Francisco Botanical Garden

(B)- Missouri Botanical Garden

(C)- Chicago Botanic Garden

(D)- Kenilworth Park and Aquatic Gardens

337- The Fuqua Orchid Center is at this location.

(A)- Majorelle Garden

(B)- UNAM Botanical Garden

(C)- The Butchart Gardens

(D)- Atlanta Botanical Garden

338- This place was inaugurated on October 12, 1989.

(A)- Yeomiji Botantical Garden

(B)- Ho'omaluhia Botanical Garden

(C)- Sarius Palmetum Botanical Garden

(D)- National Botanical Gardens (Uganda)

339- The largest concentrated collection of bonsai trees in the world is at this location.

(A)- Jerusalem Botanical Gardens

(B)- Fairchild Tropical Botanic Garden

(C)- South Coast Botanic Garden

(D)- Mauritius National Botanical Garden

340- This place has the world's largest single-span glasshouse, measuring 360 ft long and 200 ft wide.

(A)- Fondation Monet in Giverny

(B)- Lisbon Tropical Botanical Garden

(C)- National Botanic Garden of Wales

(D)- Dallas Arboretum and Botanical Garden

341- The Hartman Prehistoric Garden is at this location.

(A)- Kremenets Botanical Garden

(B)- Arboretum Nacional

(C)- Niagara Parks Botanical Gardens

(D)- Zilker Botanical Garden

342- The arboretum here contains one of the largest collections of non-indigenous champion trees in the region.

(A)- Botanical Garden St. Gallen

(B)- National Kandawgyi Botanical Gardens

(C)- Flamingo Gardens

(D)- National Cactus and Succulent Botanical Garden and Research Centre

343- Its greenhouse production facility has received Platinum certification, the first and only greenhouse to be certified.

(A)- Crossrail Place Roof Garden

(B)- Phipps Conservatory and Botanical Gardens

(C)- Jevremovac Botanical Garden

(D)- Hauck Botanic Gardens

344- This is a Green Flag Award-winning Park that contains more than 800 trees belonging to 65 species.

(A)- Baldha Garden

(B)- Franklin Park Conservatory and Botanical Gardens

(C)- Mounts Botanical Garden

(D)- The Arboretum (Nottingham)

345- At this location, they have a rock garden, a rose garden, cactus gardens, and a lotus pond.

(A)- Orman Garden

(B)- Royal Botanic Gardens, Trinidad

(C)- Johannesburg Botanical Garden

(D)- Botanical Garden of the Comenius University

Botanical Gardens (Answers)

321- C

322- B

323- C

324- A

325- C

326- B

327- D

328- A

329- D

330- B

331- D

332- C

333- A

334- A

335- C

336- B

337- D

338- A

339- A

340- C

341- D

342- C

343- B

344- D

345- A

Mixed Part 2

346- This place was established in 1853.

(A)- Benguet

(B)- Abbottabad District

(C)- Kennebec County, Maine

(D)- La Fortuna, San Carlos

347- On June 22, 2014, this place became the 1000th site to be officially inscribed on the UNESCO World Heritage List.

(A)- Band-e-Amir National Park

(B)- Perito Moreno Glacier

(C)- Okavango Delta

(D)- Monarch Butterfly Biosphere Reserve

348- On May 11, 1976, this place was designated as a U.S. National Historic Landmark District.

(A)- Half Dome

(B)- Silver Bank

(C)- Shawnee National Forest

(D)- Paterson Great Falls National Historical Park

349- The Muscogee Nation is headquartered in ....

(A)- Mineral Point, Wisconsin

(B)- Wahoo, Nebraska

(C)- Council Bluffs, Iowa

(D)- Okmulgee, Oklahoma

350- Which one has been recognized as an Important Bird Area (IBA) by BirdLife International?

(A)- San Antonio River Walk

(B)- Kahena Black Sand Beach

(C)- Sistema Dos Ojos

(D)- Chesterfield Islands

351- What County is Yellow Springs in?

(A)- Greene County, Ohio

(B)- Warren County, Ohio

(C)- Holmes County, Ohio

(D)- Lorain County, Ohio

352- Which place was part of the Minidoka Project?

(A)- Hubbard Glacier

(B)- Yenice Dam

(C)- Fortuna Glacier

(D)- Island Park Dam

353- This place is in Austria.

(A)- Waterfalls of Damajagua

(B)- Cheonjeyeon Waterfalls

(C)- Cedar Rock Falls

(D)- Fallbachfall Waterfall

354- The World Meteorological Organization established this location as the highest non-tornadic wind gust ever recorded, at 253 mph, when it occurred on April 10, 1996.

(A)- Socotra Archipelago, Yemen

(B)- Bora Bora

(C)- Barrow Island (Western Australia)

(D)- Pisgah National Forest

355- This place was founded on December 5, 1887.

(A)- Varadero

(B)- Puerto Rico Trench

(C)- Black Rock Desert

(D)- Laguna Colorada

356- The Giant's Causeway is an area of about 40,000 interlocking basalt columns. This unique landscape is located at this location.

(A)- County Antrim

(B)- County Clare

(C)- Keweenaw County

(D)- Kaua'i County

357- This place was formerly known as Mount McKinley National Park.

(A)- White Mountain National Forest

(B)- Denali National Park and Preserve

(C)- Torres del Paine National Park

(D)- Plitvice Lakes National Park

358- In 2010, the regional gross domestic product was 4,029 million euros in this area.

(A)- Province of Palawan

(B)- Hormuz Island

(C)- Daniel Campos Province

(D)- Ionian Islands

359- Which place is in Malaysia?

(A)- Wulingyuan Scenic Area

(B)- Cameron Highlands

(C)- Kaymakli Underground City

(D)- Monteverde Cloud Forest Reserve

360- As of June 2022, the estimated permanent resident population is 2,330.

(A)- Machu Picchu

(B)- Kaikōura

(C)- Quảng Nam

(D)- Oslob

361- The surface area here is 160,000 square miles.

(A)- West Maui Mountains

(B)- Beihai Park

(C)- Gulf of Aden

(D)- Malé

362- The Cibuco Swamp is located here.

(A)- Gablenz, Saxony

(B)- Sayulita

(C)- Vega Baja, Puerto Rico

(D)- Dire Dawa

363- This location is in Honshū, Japan.

(A)- Isle of Wight

(B)- Reynisdrangar

(C)- Ise-Shima National Park

(D)- Ullensvang

364- Which place was established in September 1985?

(A)- Comayagua

(B)- Costa del Sol

(C)- Chame District

(D)- Cocora Valley

365- Valley of Stars is located here.

(A)- Monte Solaro

(B)- Qeshm Island

(C)- Bird's Head Peninsula

(D)- Blowing Rock, North Carolina

366- This place hosts 32 species of wild mammals, 200 species of birds, and 500 species of plants.

(A)- Haleakalā National Park

(B)- Al Shouf Cedar Nature Reserve

(C)- Agasthyamala Biosphere Reserve

(D)- Ngong Hills

367- Veracruz, Mexico is a city sister with ....

(A)- Quetzaltenango

(B)- Varenna, Italy

(C)- Cayo Saetia

(D)- Dorado, Puerto Rico

368- The town Tasiilaq is in ....

(A)- Malta

(B)- Greenland

(C)- Uzbekistan

(D)- Curaçao

369- This place was established in 1933.

(A)- Bled, Slovenia

(B)- Lion Sands Reserve

(C)- Palo Duro Canyon

(D)- Hallstatt, Austria

370- On May 21, 1971, this place was added to the New Mexico State Register of Cultural Properties.

(A)- El Morro National Monument

(B)- Islas Marietas National Park

(C)- Dorrigo National Park

(D)- Malay Archipelago

371- This waterfall is 105 meters high.

(A)- Tamul Waterfall

(B)- Gitgit Waterfall

(C)- Fukiware Falls

(D)- Kanto Lampo Waterfall

372- Which one is called the "Big Falls"?

(A)- Stony Creek Falls

(B)- Issaqueena Falls

(C)- Bomod-ok Falls

(D)- Looking Glass Falls

373- This is one of the most popular tourist designations in Vietnam.

(A)- Iao Valley

(B)- Tabuelan

(C)- Da Lat

(D)- Trelawny Parish

374- The Kenya Wildlife Service is the Governing body for this location.

(A)- Puerto Princesa

(B)- Marsabit National Park

(C)- Tibesti Mountains

(D)- Tswalu Kalahari Reserve

375- On June 17, 1954, this place was renamed.

(A)- El Nido, Palawan

(B)- Saona Island

(C)- Port Royal Cays

(D)- Oranjestad, Aruba

376- Approximately 68 percent of land here is classified as forestland.

(A)- Providence of Sassari

(B)- Snohomish County, Washington

(C)- Tustin, California

(D)- Noosa Heads, Queensland

377- The Historic Square is located here.

(A)- Stone Mountain

(B)- Forest Preserve District of Cook County

(C)- Mount Damavand

(D)- White Oak Creek (Brown County, Ohio)

378- Which two aren't in Switzerland?

(A)- Piz Bernina & Monte Lema

(B)- Dent Blanche & Rigi

(C)- Schynige Platte & Harder Kulm

(D)- Njesuthi & Simonsberg

379- This is the world's largest single drop waterfall.

(A)- Rogie Falls

(B)- Glen Ellis Falls

(C)- Wallaman Falls

(D)- Kaieteur Falls

380- Which place is in Colombia?

(A)- Ginnie Springs

(B)- Bavarian Alps

(C)- Lake Guatavita

(D)- Guadiaro River

381- This place has 440 acres and in 1996 it became an IUCN Category III protected area.

(A)- Arches National Park

(B)- Blue Eye, Albania

(C)- Lake Muskoka

(D)- Mount Charleston

382- Which falls longest drop is 542 ft?

(A)- Cummins Falls

(B)- Multnomah Falls

(C)- Dunn's River Falls

(D)- Manabezho Falls

383- Since 1946, this place has been part of the state of Rhineland-Palatinate.

(A)- Cochem

(B)- Nitra

(C)- Bacalar

(D)- Fatick

384- This place is known for its vast white desert.

(A)- Lac Vieux Desert Indian Reservation

(B)- Daigo-ji Kyoto, Japan

(C)- Salinas Grandes

(D)- High Falls State Park

385- In 2010, this place became the European Capital of Culture.

(A)- Pécs, Hungary

(B)- Linz, Austria

(C)- Salamanca, Spain

(D)- Matera, Italy

386- The population here is 24,500.

(A)- Lofoten Archipelago, Norway

(B)- Cave-In-Rock, Illinois

(C)- Sekondi-Takoradi, Ghana

(D)- Albury, Australia

387- In 2012, which place was designated as a UNESCO World Heritage Site.

(A)- Gangwon Province

(B)- Otago, New Zealand

(C)- Máncora, Peru

(D)- Rabat, Morocco

388- Which one is in Wisconsin?

(A)- Slide Rock State Park

(B)- Meramec Caverns

(C)- Malad Gorge State Park

(D)- Cave of the Mounds

389- This place is famous for its olive groves.

(A)- Qabatiya

(B)- Sakonnet Garden

(C)- Yorkshire Dales

(D)- Kenroku-en

390- Which place isn't in Canada?

(A)- Dinosaur Provincial Park

(B)- Dún na Rí Forest Park

(C)- Athabasca Sand Dunes Provincial Park

(D)- Auyuittuq National Park

391- This place is nicknamed the "Butterfly Island" because of its shape.

(A)- Faroe Islands, Denmark

(B)- Havelock Island

(C)- Kaho'olawe

(D)- Astypalea

392- This place was established on October 11, 1934.

(A)- Tel Dan Nature Reserve

(B)- The Wilds (Ohio)

(C)- Babcock State Park

(D)- Macaw Mountain Bird Park & Nature Reserve

393- The length of this river is 135 miles.

(A)- Nišava

(B)- Chaliyar

(C)- Ryesŏng River

(D)- Mekong River

394- The Wilderness Society has designated the area as a "Mountain Treasure."

(A)- Devils Island (Wisconsin)

(B)- Devils Fork (Conservation Area)

(C)- Devil's Den State Park

(D)- Devil's Icebox (Cave)

395- In 2020, the population here was around 1,650.

(A)- Banjul, Gambia

(B)- Guacalito De La Isla, Nicaragua

(C)- Lookout Mountain, Georgia

(D)- Hatta, United Arab Emirates

396- Which place isn't in Oregon?

(A)- Bagby Hot Springs

(B)- Cape Perpetua

(C)- Lava River Cave

(D)- Mammoth Cave National Park

397- This place is in Russia.

(A)- Matanuska Glacier

(B)- Tsitsikamma National Park

(C)- Montgomery Bell Tunnel

(D)- Valley of Geysers

398- This place is in the northwestern province of Estuaire.

(A)- Los Patos, Dominican Republic

(B)- Saint Mary Parish, Jamaica

(C)- Libreville, Gabon

(D)- Parkland Region, Manitoba

399- This site was added to the World Heritage List in 1980.

(A)- Copán

(B)- Maracas Valley

(C)- Jacob's Well

(D)- Trilobite Quarry

400- Naqsh-e Jahan Square at this location is one of the largest city squares in the world.

(A)- Palmyra

(B)- Ladakh

(C)- Takesi

(D)- Isfahan

Mixed Part 2 (Answers)

346- B

347- C

348- D

349- D

350- D

351- A

352- D

353- D

354- C

355- A

356- A

357- B

358- D

359- B

360- B

361- C

362- C

363- C

364- D

365- B

366- B

367- A

368- B

369- B

370- A

371- A

372- C

373- C

374- B

375- A

376- B

377- A

378- D

379- D

380- C

381- B

382- B

383- A

384- C

385- A

386- A

387- D

388- D

389- A

390- B

391- D

392- C

393- A

394- B

395- C

396- D

397- D

398- C

399- A

400- D

(List of My Books)

Successful Professional Gamblers

The Neighborhood Competition

Trivia About Occupations

Trivia About Politics

True or False: 5 Categories Edition

True or False: 2024 Olympics & Paralympics Edition

True or False: Organizing & Movements Edition

True or False: Powerchair Football & Power Soccer Edition

True or False: Video Games & esports Edition

Women in College Sports Trivia

Women in Sports Trivia

Worldwide Locations Trivia

My Email: LanceCares@gmail.com